Wisdom Keys

Phyllis Clemmons

McClure Publishing, Inc.

Copyright © 2014

All rights reserved. Printed and bound in the United States of America. According to the 1976 United States Copyright Act, no part of this book may be reproduced or utilized in any form or by any means, electronic or mechanical, including photocopying, recording, or by any information storage or retrieval system, except by a reviewer who may quote brief passages in a review to be printed in a magazine or newspaper, without permission in writing from the Publisher: Inquiries should be addressed to McClure Publishing, Inc. Permissions Department, Bloomingdale, Illinois. Publication date: April 1, 2014.

Scripture reference is taken from the King James Version (KJV) of the Bible.

The author and publisher have made every effort to ensure the accuracy and completeness of information contained in this book, we assume no responsibility for errors, inaccuracies, omissions, or any inconsistencies therein.

ISBN: 978-09915335-8-9
LCCN: 2014937334

Cover background ID: 5328375 (123rf.com)
Image of the Lock and Keys from Etsy
Interior Book Block Design: Kathy McClure

Order Copies of Wisdom Keys at
www.mcclurepublishing.com

INTRODUCTION

First and foremost, let me begin by clarifying the significance of doors and keys. One of the promises of God says, "The thief cometh not, but for to steal, and to kill, and to destroy: I am come that they might have life, and that they might have it more abundantly." (John 10:10 KJV). These promises are given to believers. Those who have unlocked and opened the most important door, which is the door to their heart and invites Jesus to come in, will be free. This single act is the beginning of the most powerful and needful relationship and fellowship available to mankind.

In Revelation 3:20 there is a written invitation that reads,

"Behold, I stand at the door, and knock: if any man hear my voice, and open the door, I will come in to him, and will sup with him, and he with me." I came across an article on the website at www.biblestudytools.com that said, "The Middle Eastern code of ethics held strongly to a belief that good hospitality was the command of The Divine, and the offer to partake of a meal was a sacred, holy and consecrated act."

A website called OpenBible.info under the Topical Bible section lists 23 scriptures about doors. (I have listed them all in the back of this booklet for further study and reflection). There, I found something interesting. Among the 23 scriptures mentioned, all of them had the word "door" in them with the exception of, I Timothy 2:8. This passage says, "I will therefore that men pray every where…." Nevertheless, the word "door" was not mentioned anywhere in this passage of scripture or any other passage listed before or after this scripture within that chapter. At first I thought it odd and contemplated leaving it out but after reading it again, it occurred to me that the subject of this verse is prayer. It brought to mind that prayer is an open door access to God. Before Christ died on the cross for our sins, we were not able to go to God for ourselves. During the lifetime of Jesus, the holy temple in Jerusalem was the center of Jewish religious life. The temple was the place where animal sacrifices were carried out and worship according to the Law of Moses was followed faithfully. Hebrews 9:1-9 tells us that in the temple a veil separated the Holy of Holies (the earthly dwelling place of God's presence) from the rest of the temple where men dwelt. This signified that man was separated from God by sin (Isaiah 59:1-2). Only the high priest was permitted to pass beyond this veil once each year (Exodus 30:10; Hebrews 9:7) to enter into God's presence for all of Israel and make atonement for their sins (Leviticus 16).

Matthew 27:51 says, "And, behold, the veil of the temple was rent in twain (two parts) from the top to the bottom...." Christ's death and atonement for our sins was the key that unlocked the door to direct access to Him. It granted us entrance into the Holy of Holies so that we can now ask forgiveness for our sins as well as bring all other prayers and petitions before God.

This Companion booklet is based on my journey in *Kelsey from Pain to Triumph* and by example of my own life, it is my hope that it will give insight to how the pain of many of the obstacles that I faced as a young girl could have been diminished and in some cases completely eliminated if I had known how to effectively handle the situations I now share with you.

Although, the key that unlocks the door to salvation as well as the key that unlocks the door to prayer got me through to a triumphant conclusion, when you are only working with one or two keys, you end up not getting to your destination by the most effective and shortest route possible. It is my desire to share with you some of the methods of operation that could have been accomplished in a more excellent way if I had utilized the third key.

This is the key that unlocks the door of knowledge and wisdom by way of reading and studying the Bible and referenced by the Holy Spirit to instruct us on proper application of what the Bible teaches. (John 14:26 KJV).

Without this key, you will often not only find yourself in unfavorable situations, but you will also find that you can stay in that difficulty for a much longer period of time.

It is my hope that you will use my journey based on my book, *Kelsey from Pain to Triumph*, as well as this companion booklet as an analogy and example of how you too will be able to come to a triumphant conclusion, in addition to receiving God's absolute best for your future.

INSTRUCTIONS

Start by reading each day and meditate on that day before moving to the next day. After reaching Day 31, start all over again for an entire year to see how *WISDOM KEYS* will take you to a higher level of maturity.

WISDOM KEYS
based on my book:
Kelsey from Pain to Triumph

WISDOM KEYS

Day 1

I will cut right to the chase. This booklet of Wisdom Keys is not designed to feed you mini meals that are not pleasant to your palate. Nevertheless, it is not feasible that I can serve you a healthy yet scrumptious mini meal and leave out the main course. However, I promise to do my best not to force feed you anything that is unsavory for your consumption.

On that note, let me say, I love to taste delicious and healthy food but I always deplored okra! As a young girl I had no choice. It was mandatory in our house to eat what was put before us, so my plight with okra began as a discipline. As the years went by,

there would be good cooks that would attempt to convince me that they could make okra in such a way, that I would love it. This declaration was a motivation to my curiosity and gave me a desire to try other preparation methods to determine if I would like it any better. Then one day, I tried okra cut up in small bite sized pieces, well-seasoned and sautéed in a light, crispy batter. Surprisingly, I found it to be delightful! After practicing eating this healthy vegetable prepared in different ways, what started as a **discipline** changed to **desire** and then to **delight**.

To some, the things of God that bring good health to your spirit is like okra, it is best for you but may not please your appetite at first. Although it is the main

WISDOM KEYS

course of the meal, you have my word that I will serve it to you in small bite size pieces, seasoned so that it will be a savory delight to your spiritual palate.

WISDOM KEYS

Day 2

Beloved, before you make any hasty or rash decisions, remember that it can have a devastating and extremely long term adverse effect on your life. If something sounds too good to be true, it probably is. Take the time to think things through, exploring all of the possible ramifications of your decisions (at least the ones that you know of). Talk it over with a confidant, someone that you have the highest regard for their wise counsel. Don't just jump out there all willy nilly before careful consideration of the facts at hand. Also remember that bad decisions come with serious and painful consequences.

WISDOM KEYS

Day 3

Fears of loneliness, of the unknown, of retaliation, etc., can keep us from removing ourselves from an abusive relationship.

Back in the day, there was a cartoon character whose name was Snagglepuss and whenever he recognized danger was near he would say, "Exit stage right," and immediately he would make a speedy departure.

Whenever you have reached a conclusion that you are in an unhealthy and dangerously abusive relationship, start planning. Begin watching for doors to open to an escape route and when it presents itself, "Exit stage right!" Afraid? You can still take action in

WISDOM KEYS

the midst of fear. As long as you can see the first step, you can start walking. As Martin Luther King said, "You don't have to see the whole staircase to take the first step."

WISDOM KEYS

Day 4

As a child, I remember following the example of an older relative. As a result, I became violently ill. Keep in mind, what you pass down through your actions is being observed by others that look up to you. Recognize that the choices you make can adversely affect future generations to come.

Wisdom Keys

Day 5

Sometimes life will show us just a glimmer of the silver lining of a cloud so that we do not lose hope because hope does not disappoint.

The gravitational force reaches its full acceleration when something or someone is either pushed, thrown or falls to the extreme bottom. What I always liked about hope is, when you roll back the curtain on your own personal life experiences, you are able to see that the circumstantial seasons of life are continually going up and down, unceasingly changing.

You can be slammed down prostrate to the valley floor one minute by the gravitational pull

WISDOM KEYS

brought on by the difficulties of life (whether they are gradual or instantaneous), change can take place, and suddenly you are standing up straight and tall looking eyeball to eyeball with the highest mountain peak. Therefore, I know that whenever I'm in a valley season, I can encourage myself that there is nowhere else to go but up. A CHANGE IS GOING TO COME!

WISDOM KEYS

Day 6

In these modern days and times, things have changed drastically since I was a teenager. Back then, whenever a young lady met a young man that showed interest in her and she also was attracted to him, there would be an exchange of telephone numbers between the two so that dialogue between them could continue. Sometimes, the young man did not call as soon as anticipated, sometimes, he did not call at all. However, no matter how much you wanted that dialogue to continue, it was a cardinal rule that the young lady **could not, should not and would not make the call!**

WISDOM KEYS

It was the custom of that day that the man be the pursuer. You understood that the young man enjoyed the hunt and the hunt is part of what makes you more interesting to him. It is the part that motivates him because it presents a challenge for him to work at. Whenever the young lady would attempt to pursue, through initiated telephone contact, going to his home, etc. she was actually taking away that part of the challenge that the young man loved most, the pursuit and intrigue. The young man would often lose interest and cease to be captivated. I'm saying all this to say, young ladies; **slow your role.**

WISDOM KEYS

Day 7

Sometimes our child rearing techniques are out of balance. Mainly because in most cases, we do not attend classes, read books or see examples that give us good sound guidance on the subject. Therefore, we find ourselves using the techniques that our parents or guardians used in rearing us. The cycle continues from generation to generation. This is a form of a generational curse.

Extremely severe punishments are often unequal to the level of misconduct displayed. If you have not always gotten what you deserved, consider this: Why not sprinkle a little grace and mercy on the opposite side of the gauge

sometimes? It just might balance the scale enough to bring that child into proper alignment.

WISDOM KEYS

Day 8

I am elated that schools begin the practice of "show and tell" as early as pre-kindergarten. It teaches children how, to not only show a cherished item that they have chosen and brought from home but also teaches them to demonstrate how to operate that item. It also helps them to understand at an early age the benefit of verbal instructions as well as demonstration of the process as well. Although we are all created equal, our brains are unique and function differently.

Some people can just hear the instructions on how to do something and grasp it immediately. Some people

comprehend it better when they are shown how it operates and some must hear the instruction and see how it functions in order to get a clear understanding of how it works. I am in the very last category, needing both audio and visual instructions before full revelation is manifested in my mind.

One example of the importance of show and tell is the act of love. Although you may be told that you are loved, if you are not shown the affection of one who is loved; it does not fully resonate and therefore, looks like an oxymoron (something that contradicts information). Its verbal connotation is the opposite of the actual display of emotion that is shown.

WISDOM KEYS

Many mothers will one day be great grandmothers. The legacy that you want to leave to the generations that follow you, is one that shows love and affection to our children so that they have an example to show to their children and will also be passed down to their children's children. We cannot show what we have not been shown. Let us begin to break old dysfunctional habits by showing love not only in words but also in deeds.

WISDOM KEYS

Day 9

One day we are here and the next day we may be gone. It has been said that we are a temporary vapor. Once the smoke disintegrates, people come to say goodbye and talk about their fondest memories of you. Something you did or something you said that they carry in their hearts and minds.

Once they are no longer able to smell your fragrance or audibly hear the words that were unique to you or feel the embrace of your warm body accompanied by your greeting or fond goodbye, the memory of your essence will begin to fade as time goes by. What you say and do in this life matters!

Only the history of the famous remain naturally for years to come as they have the magazine articles, books and written documentation of their deeds, (both good and bad) left behind to provoke the memory of their former existence.

We must endeavor to leave a strong deposit in the earth that invokes the corners of lips to turn upward as the memory of your encouraging and loving words once spoken and periodically come to mind just at the right time, or the pride that is felt when thoughts of your prior deeds are still talked about that say to those who admired you, I too can do this.

Do not fail to bring meaning to your life that will last forever. We

WISDOM KEYS

may not become world famous, but we all must be remembered and honored by all those that we have encountered for the sake of a good and lasting deposit left behind in the earth.

WISDOM KEYS

Day 10

Be careful who you connect yourself with. Negative role models do not enhance your life for good and whatever is on them has a way of rubbing off on you. Always seek to build relationships with those who are a positive addition and influence to your life. Remember, who others are, and what they do will affect you. You may be innocent, but deemed guilty by association.

Choose your friends wisely. Understand, there is no shame in being alone and it, by no means constitutes loneliness. Learn to be comfortable in your own skin and enjoy your own company.

WISDOM KEYS

Day 11

Sometimes we can make decisions that ultimately create a mess in our lives. As we do, we think to ourselves that what we are doing doesn't affect anyone else. We tell ourselves that we are not hurting anyone.

After one such episode in my own life, I made the decision to do something without any regard, consideration or forethought to how it would affect others. The end result was that I made a complete mess of things that were left for someone else to clean up. Think before you act! The consequences of the things that you do often trickle down and the unpleasant residuals are left for others to clean up.

WISDOM KEYS

Day 12

Take the time and the care to be an auditor of your words before you permit your thoughts to escape the doors of your lips. Decrees of negative proclamations spoken over the lives of others can cause a corresponding reaction to the very thing you have expressed over their lives.

Don't speak **words** over someone, that are a reflection of the negative behavior patterns and characteristics that appear to be at work in them, but speak positive patterns of behavior and characteristics you hope for.

The human psyche is motivated by and responsive to all

affirmations whether they are positive or negative.

WISDOM KEYS

Day 13

Maya Angelou once said, "No lesson is learned immediately." We all understand on a certain level, but a lesson given over and over again brings deeper understanding each time.

As a preteen, the lessons that presented themselves were more simplistic in nature. As a teen and a young adult the lessons of life became more complex and required me to take what I had learned in earlier lessons and build on them.

It is much the same as an Algebraic math problem. The first time I took beginners Algebra, I discovered that each lesson is a stepping stone to the next lesson.

WISDOM KEYS

It is imperative that you learn the foundational rules given in the first lesson. You could not make sense of the future lesson levels if you did not learn the foundational rules as they started to build upon each other in succession, causing an increase in complexity.

For each life example that occurs, you must ask yourself at that time, "What can I learn from this situation?" Then use what you have learned to build upon the next lesson. It is impossible to learn the complexities of life when you have not first mastered the simplicities of life.

WISDOM KEYS

Day 14

Abraham Lincoln ran for public office many times and lost. He was a very persistent man that never gave up. Eventually, he would become the 16th President of the United States.

If you have a dream and it does not appear to be coming to fruition, don't give up on the dream but approach it from a different perspective. Ponder over it daily. Think about why it may not be working. Sometimes it could be that you are operating outside of God's timing. Some revelations present themselves early as a foretaste of things to come. Time and seasons are important. You may be trying to make something work that is

WISDOM KEYS

ahead of its time. The dream may require some preparation on your part before it can materialize.

Do all you can to prepare yourself for a positive out-come. Believe that the precise moment will present itself when opportunity and preparation will come into alignment simultaneously, then seize the moment and go for it!

WISDOM KEYS

Day 15

Pride always places blame on someone else. Its mind is unchangeable to a fault. Its spirit is unteachable to the highest degree. It is unwavering in its convictions. It is blind to its own flaws and weaknesses. It refuses to acknowledge the truth even when truth is irrefutable. It twistedly and relentlessly stays focused on having its own way and cannot be reasoned with, even when the evidence points to a conclusion that is different from its own. At all cost, it justifies its position and never, ever admits when it is wrong. It is numb to shame and leaves no room for humility. It is foolish to become companions with it.

WISDOM KEYS

Day 16

Be encouraged! Your finest hour has not yet come. Know without a shadow of doubt, that your start does not determine your finish by any means. Stop using your past as a measuring stick by which you see into your future.

You can't change what has already been documented in your life's history, so forget about it! Change your direction on the map of life by making good, sound, calculated decisions that are designed to get you to the destination of a better future.

You may experience some detours along the way but you can recover, get back on course and never give up on yourself!

WISDOM KEYS

Day 17

Robert Baden-Powell said that "Correcting bad habits cannot be done by forbidding or punishment." Normally, breaking bad habits takes a considerable amount of conscious effort, discipline and time to eradicate. Unhealthy learned behaviors cannot be erased overnight. After all, they have been consistently embedded in your memory by repetitive use over a period of time.

Begin to commit to a daily practice of correction in one area in order to erase what has been recorded over an extended period of time in your memory bank. Do not attempt to give yourself a complete overhaul by striving to

correct all of your flawed areas all at once. Start by correcting one thing at a time and stay with it until that which you have practiced becomes second nature to you. Also, it is good to have one confidant who will help you to be accountable in your efforts and to encourage you when you fall down in that area, to get back up and keep moving forward until you have mastered each weak area one day at a time, one step at a time and one flaw at a time.

WISDOM KEYS

Day 18

An early 1950's movie called *The Three Faces of Eve* is the story of a young woman who developed a multiple personality disorder due to a traumatic event that happened to her as a six year old child. I closely relate to this story as I too experienced a similar traumatic event at the age of 6 years old. I didn't develop the same mental illness that Eve did, but I definitely went through some deep emotional distress for a long period of time as a result of that trauma.

In both scenarios, the traumatic event was avoidable. The trauma took place as a result of a decision made by a parent. Parents' discernment is a vital

WISDOM KEYS

instinct. If not correctly judged, it can cause our children to experience unnecessary distress and lead to long term unhealthy emotional disturbances. There are situations that occur that an adult mind has the ability to apply sound reasoning and understanding to. However, a child's mind, due to lack of understanding, could develop fears if exposed to the same type of situations. (It is common to experience fear of the unknown). Be careful not to expose your children to situations that can leave long lasting emotional ramifications.

WISDOM KEYS

Day 19

I often have trouble letting go of relationships that have been a positive influence in my life or the memory of relationships that bring back warm fuzzy feelings within me. It took me a long time to understand that many people will come into your life for a specific moment in time. When that time is over, they will move on and may never be heard from again.

There were times when I would try my best to find and rekindle such relationships as they brought joy to my life, when they were a part of my life. Whenever I tried, often the door to renewing that relationship would be closed and no matter how I

tried, I was unable to pry it open again. This lesson has taught me that people will come into your life and many will be removed from your life when that season of your relationship is over. Do not pursue! They have already fulfilled the requirement that they were sent to accomplish.

WISDOM KEYS

Day 20

When crabs are harvested, the crabs as a group will pull down any crab that starts to climb out of the barrel.

This reminds me of how misery loves company. She is unsatisfied when she is by herself and is comforted only by her ability to pull someone down to her same emotional level, provoking a miserable experience very much like her own. She has a twisted, temporary relief whenever she is generously dishing out huge servings of her suffering to anyone who crosses her path. She enjoys and welcomes the company of others as she derives great pleasure from sharing her distress and discomforts with

WISDOM KEYS

anyone and everyone she comes in contact with. If it is within your power, do not keep company with her.

WISDOM KEYS

Day 21

Life can and will throw you a curve ball from time to time. Don't panic! When you are faced with a curve ball, don't look at it as if it were an unbeatable opponent. It has been said that we only use a small fraction of our mind's capacity. We have the extraordinary ability to be great problem solvers. Yet, most of our thoughts barely scratch the surface of its aptitude. We resist the struggle to think deeper. Have enough faith to know that extraordinary gifts and potential has already been placed inside of you. With God as our help, nothing is impossible for you.

WISDOM KEYS

Day 22

It has been said that experience is the best teacher. Probably because if you don't feel the discomfort from mistakes you have made, you are very likely to make the same mistakes again. For example, if you put your hand over a hot flame it will burn you. The burn will be painful, therefore, you have experienced the pain from the hot flame. The next time you see the hot flame, you will remember the pain it caused. The lesson learned from such a painful mistake is to warn us of the danger of a repeat performance as well as teach us a lesson that will help us to develop and grow.

WISDOM KEYS

Day 23

While on my morning exercise run, I was strongly overtaken by a concept in "letter" style.

INTRODUCTION:

A brief lesson on a few definitions that will contribute to making wiser relationship decisions:

BODY/MAIN IDEA:

1. The phrase, "Out of Order" means that something or someone is not operating in the manner in which it, he or she was designed to function.

2. It has been said, that one meaning of the word "Intimacy" means 'Into Me See'.

WISDOM KEYS

Many times our relationship "order" is out of whack. Perhaps you and your mate have chosen to see into each other sexually before purposing to see into each other: Spiritually, as well as mentally and intellectually. First, learning personalities, character traits or moral standards of each other, helps to keep the relationship in alignment.

We are multi-faceted people. Dig deeper! Beneath the surface is where you see into the real person that dwells on the inside of that eye catching outer shell.

CONCLUSION:

Pay attention to likes and dislikes of your mate, pay attention to habits, characteristics, unhealthy emotions and the effects of

WISDOM KEYS

baggage dragged along from previous relationships.

Ask yourself these questions: is he or she productive in a positive way? Does he or she work or go to school? Is he or she active in community service or volunteer work, etc.? It can eliminate much heartache later on. Pay attention to red flags and warning signs that do not set well in your mind or spirit.

WISDOM KEYS

Day 24

I believe, when we make our grand entrance into the world at birth, although we are diminutive in physical stature on arrival, we come in at our fullest, fat with purpose and promise. As we experience life and mature, a steady stream should be pouring out of us. That stream should consist of love, compassion, prayers for others, healing words, knowledge, gifts, service, skills, encouraging words, hugs and all that constitutes blessings toward others.

When you leave this earth, you should leave empty of all the good that was placed inside of you in order to leave the earth in

a better condition than when you entered it.

This should always be the goal and legacy of every man, woman, boy and girl, to leave behind a deposit of seeds to stimulate a lavish and plush garden whose soil is rich with fertilizer that is intended to promote spiritual, physical, financial, emotional and mental wealth, as well as healthy and extravagant beauty throughout the earth.

Day 25

When I was younger, I use to think that money was the most valuable commodity that we could have. As years have gone by, I have adopted a different philosophy. Time is by far, more superior in significance and importance.

Come! Let us embrace the day that we have been blessed by God to share in. Each new day that we can bring comfort to a distressed life, joy where there is sorrow, prayer for a sin sick soul, encouragement and hope for tomorrow, will make this world a better place.

While we still remain, we have the ability to generate and impart something good into the lives of

WISDOM KEYS

others. Otherwise, as each day passes, so also is the passing of missed opportunities. There is a price to be paid for each day that goes by that you have left barren without adding value to the lives of those that you could have touched in a positive way.

Take charge of the day while it is still day to leave a good and fertile deposit before entering into tomorrow.

WISDOM KEYS

Day 26

There is a popular advertisement slogan that states that a Timex® watch can take a licking and keep on ticking. I found myself curious as to how this particular name brand watch has been able to survive and thrive throughout the years among so many popular name brand watches that come and go. I decided to do a little research via one of the Google internet websites to see exactly what materials are used in creating this timing device that gives it such strength and durability.

This is what I found: It is flexible, it promotes comfort, embodies dependability, has a strong frame that is shaped with steel and it is

sealed with a stain resistant material. It keeps perfect time.

Its padded casing helps to eliminate irritation and provides unexpected style, (which is the method or approach used to do something). Its element resistant pieces survive every depth. Rubber braids and nylon bands adapt to cold. Mineral crystals defend against damage. Metallic casings shield the mechanics, (which are the functional and technical aspects of the device).

Friction is the arch enemy of precision timekeeping as well as an enemy to many other things. Precision is the watches ability to be accurate over time and through a variety of conditions.

I remember thinking to myself that those who manufactured such a piece, took the time and

WISDOM KEYS

loving care to put everything into it that was needed to buffet every type of element it would or could encounter.

We also have a Creator and when we put our lives into his hands, He first seals us with the Holy Spirit and then puts everything inside of us that is necessary to equip us to buffet every kind of possible friction or difficulty we could or would face in order to live in precision with the plan that has been ordained for our lives.

WISDOM KEYS

Day 27

Nielson's Newswire states that Thomas Edison, one of America's greatest inventors and world renown for his invention of the light bulb had a learning experience. One of Edison's failures taught him the important relationship between invention and marketing.

In 1869 he invented and patented an Electronic Vote Recorder to tally votes in the Massachusetts state legislature. It worked faster and more accurately. To Edison's astonishment, it was a complete flop.... Although Edison had an excellent idea, he completely misunderstood the needs of his potential customers."

WISDOM KEYS

In my youth I had many failures. I'm glad that failure does not withhold future opportunities for success. Instead, each time I failed, it eliminated what did not work so that I could redirect my focus toward a new strategy. I understand now that although the word failure sounds negative, in my estimation it is a positive educational teaching tool. Each time I fail, I ask myself, "What can I learn from this incident?" Then I seek a fresh approach to the situation.

The issues of life often require us the regular practice of being a problem solver. It has been said that, "it is insanity to repeat the exact same process and expect a different result." God's word says that I have been given a spirit of power, of love and of a sound

WISDOM KEYS

mind. Therefore, I use my mind to seek after new solutions to previous failures.

WISDOM KEYS

Day 28

Do you remember the story of the three little pigs? This story has such an influential meaning. The basic concept of the story tells a biblical truth that houses built on a firm foundation made of good strong materials are more likely to withstand the storms of life. They don't keep the storms from coming, but they keep the storms from destroying you.

Your firm foundation is the rock of ages, (His name is Jesus). When you hand over Lordship to Him, you are reborn and made into a new creature. This new creature has been made with good strong building materials. The architect of the building is

WISDOM KEYS

familiar with your frame and knows how much it can handle. He will not allow the external forces of life to blow your spiritual house down.

WISDOM KEYS

Day 29

All pain is not the consequences of unwise decisions. According to an internet article written by Property 24, the overall wellness of a garden is contingent upon regular pruning while the flowers and fruit from those plants and trees are lying dormant. This usually takes place during late winter through early spring. Some, (particularly spring blooming shrubs and trees) will start showing new buds as soon as the old buds have fallen.

Pruning is extremely beneficial, as it keeps plants strong and flowering, and it will not harm the plant in the long run.

All nature operates by laws that have been set in gesticulation (motion) by God. The law of

WISDOM KEYS

pruning works in accordance with making and keeping the blooms healthy and thick and the fruit luscious. It adds longevity and maximizes fruit as well as bloom production. It exposes the tree or shrub more evenly to light, gets rid of old dead stems and creates a new shape to that particular foliage. For example, a rose bush should be pruned in the shape of a trophy. It brings balance that will endure weight as well.

When we are in the winter season of our lives, as we lie dormant, this is the time God is cutting back and removing old or dead things, in order to bring new shape and balance, as well as fullness to new blooms that are budding in our lives.

Even though pruning is painful, it is a very necessary process. It

WISDOM KEYS

operates in us just as the laws of nature operate after its kind, so that we can become a beautiful, luscious and full garden that invites the world to see, with the hope that they will desire to become one with the Creator of the garden.

WISDOM KEYS

Day 30

Although my book is beneficial and pleasurable for all to read, I have a very strong compassion for young children, teens and young adults. A great man of God, Dr. Mike Murdock says, "Those who unlock your compassion are those to whom you have been assigned."

With that end in mind, my book *Kelsey from Pain to Triumph* is my homework assignment. It focuses on that same band of time in my own life. My hope is that I will reach some troubled heart that will read about my own journey and be encouraged and infused with new hope, renewed strength and faith as they walk through their own

WISDOM KEYS

journey of life with a fresh understanding and perspective that no matter what obstacles and painful difficulties in life they face, whether they be due to the painful consequences of poor decision making, pain as a result of the vicissitudes of life or pain as the subject of God's pruning shears, know that the Father is always aware of your situation.

His invisible hand is always moving in your life (even when you see no movement). He is always watching over you and saying, "Don't trip, I got you!"

WISDOM KEYS

Day 31

Air, water, food, and shelter are essential to our survival as well as essential for sustaining of our physical being. We can also be assured that our spirit will be sustained with the provider who is known by these names: breath of life, living water, bread of heaven and shelter in times of storm.

Our Creator has thought of everything to secure all things essential to our physical and our spiritual well-being. I am thankful to have an opportunity to serve the one who has every facet of my life under His control and care.

WISDOM KEYS

CONCLUSION:

It is my hope that *Wisdom Keys* will bring you a sense of urgency to want to walk in the wisdom mentioned inside the pages of this book. Keep in mind all the keys that I mentioned in the introduction: the **first key** opens the door of your heart to Jesus, the **second key** gives you access to Him through prayer and the **third key** opens the door to the knowledge and wisdom of God and application of His Word by the instruction of the Holy Spirit. These three keys unlock the secrets behind each door and each open door reveals a part of the road map to abundant life and to your future.

WISDOM KEYS

23 Bible Verses about Doors

1. Revelation 3:20
2. Revelation 3:8
3. Matthew 7:7
4. I Corinthians 16:8-9
5. John 10:1-42
6. Matthew 6:6
7. Psalm 24:7
8. Proverbs 8:34
9. Matthew 7:13-14
10. I Corinthians 16:9
11. Revelations 4:1
12. Acts 5:19
13. II Chronicles 29:3
14. II Kings 4:4
15. Genesis 4:7
16. James 5:9
17. II Corinthians 2:12
18. Acts 13:47
19. Psalm 14:13
20. I Timothy 2:8
21. John 10:9
23. Hosea 2:15

Author's Bio

Phyllis Clemmons holds a Bachelor's degree in Business Administration from Faulkner Christian University and a Master's Degree in Human Resource Development, Management and Leadership from Webster University. She has 45 years of combined public service work.

Phyllis has had the privilege of teaching Sunday school overseas as well as the United States. She is passionate in ministering a Godly word of encouragement to those who are sick, discouraged, down trodden and broken hearted. She has ministered in praise dancing as well as program designer for the Sisters in the Spirit Annual Retreats. She is a facilitator for her church's weekly prayer line as well as a member of the praise team.

www.ingramcontent.com/pod-product-compliance
Lightning Source LLC
Chambersburg PA
CBHW072105290426
44110CB00014B/1840